Revised Edition

Peyton Manning

By Jeff Savage

AMAZING
ATHLETES

Lerner Publications Company • Minneapolis

Lerner Publications Company
A division of Lerner Publishing Group, Inc.
241 First Avenue North
Minneapolis, MN 55401 U.S.A.

Website address: www.lernerbooks.com

Library of Congress Cataloging-in-Publication Data

Savage, Jeff, 1961–
    Peyton Manning / by Jeff Savage. — [Rev. ed.].
       p.   cm. — (Amazing athletes)
    Includes bibliographical references and index.
    ISBN-13: 978–0–8225–6445–4 (lib. bdg. : alk. paper)
    1. Manning, Peyton—Juvenile literature. 2. Football players—United States—Biography—Juvenile literature. I. Title.
    GV939.M289S27 2008
    796.332092—dc22 [B]   2007006896

Manufactured in the United States of America
1 2 3 4 5 6 – DP – 13 12 11 10 09 08

5/08

c.1

TABLE OF CONTENTS

The 2007 Super Bowl was held in Miami, Florida.

SUPER MANNING

The rain came down in sheets as Indianapolis Colts' quarterback Peyton Manning stood on the edge of the field. All around him, fans roared and cameras clicked. The Colts and the Chicago Bears were to face off in the 2007 Super Bowl. The biggest football game of the year was about to begin. Chicago's **defense** was one of the best in the NFL. Would they be good enough to stop Peyton and the Colts?

The Super Bowl did not start well for the Colts. The first play of the game was a kickoff to Chicago. The Bears ran the kick all the way back for a **touchdown**. After the extra point kick, Indianapolis was down, 7–0. When the Colts got the ball, Peyton threw an **interception** to Chicago. In the first few minutes of the game the Bears had a chance to go ahead by two touchdowns.

The Bears defense tries to stop Peyton and his team from scoring.

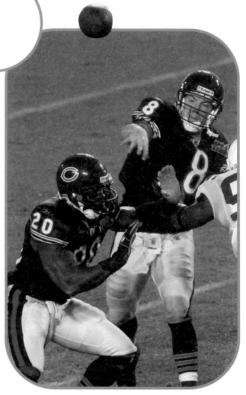

Bears' quarterback Rex Grossman *(wearing number eight)* throws a pass during the Super Bowl.

The Indianapolis defense was also tough. They swarmed Bears' quarterback Rex Grossman and kept Chicago from scoring. Peyton took the field to try to get his team back in the game. He wiped a hand across his face to clear the water from his eyes. This time Peyton was sharp. After a couple of short passes, he hurled a 53-yard toss to Reggie Wayne for a touchdown. But the Colts didn't get the extra point kick. The score was 7–6.

The Colts defense again kept the Bears from

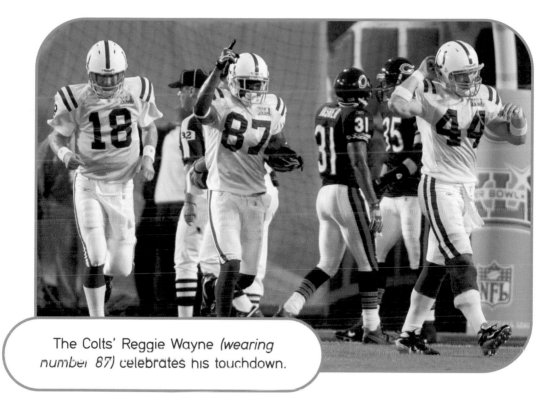

The Colts' Reggie Wayne *(wearing number 87)* celebrates his touchdown.

scoring. Indianapolis got the ball back. But the wet weather made the field and the football very slippery. The ball slipped from Peyton's hands to the ground. The tough Chicago defense jumped on the **fumble**. The Bears had another chance to score. Grossman threw a pass to Muhsin Muhammad in the **end zone**. The Bears were ahead, 14–6.

Dominic Rhodes carries the ball for the Colts.

The Colts had to fight from behind. The Chicago defense was playing very well. Would Peyton and the Colts be up to the challenge?

A Colts' field goal made the score 14–9. When Indianapolis got the ball back again, Peyton led them toward the end zone. He handed the ball to running back Dominic Rhodes near the **goal line**. Rhodes dove for the touchdown. After the extra point kick, the Colts were ahead, 16–14.

Once Indianapolis had the lead, Peyton made sure the team didn't let it go. At the end of the last quarter, Indianapolis was ahead, 29–17. Peyton and the Colts had done it. They were Super Bowl champions! Peyton was named most valuable player (MVP) of the game. "It's hard to put into words," he said after the win. "I'm proud to be part of this team."

Football is a team sport. But Colts' coach Tony Dungy knows that his star quarterback is someone special. "Peyton is a tremendous player, a great leader," Coach Dungy said. "This guy is a Hall of Fame player and one of the greatest ever to play."

Coach Dungy (center) and Peyton celebrate their Super Bowl victory.

Peyton's parents—Archie Manning and Olivia Williams—both went to the University of Mississippi. The school is nicknamed Ole Miss.

BORN TO THROW

Peyton Williams Manning was born March 24, 1976, to Archie and Olivia Manning. Olivia had been the homecoming queen at the University of Mississippi, where Archie had also been a star player. Archie had been an NFL quarterback for fourteen years, playing mostly for the New Orleans Saints.

Peyton and his brothers—Cooper and Eli—lived with their parents in New Orleans, Louisiana. They often watched their father play.

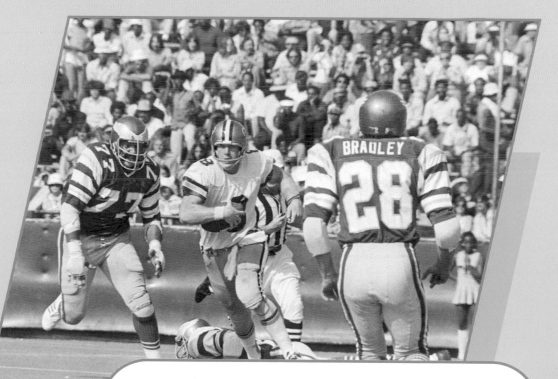

Archie (running with ball) played for the New Orleans Saints for twelve years. Even though Archie played well, the team wasn't very good during his career.

Peyton loved football from the start. By age three, he was playing the game with his father and older brother, Cooper, in the living room. Archie would carry a tiny football and try to scoot past his boys on his knees. By age four, Peyton was throwing his little football perfectly. Each Christmas, Peyton and his brothers would find gifts of helmets, jerseys, and other football gear beneath their tree. Peyton dreamed of someday being a quarterback, just like his dad.

Cooper Manning got a serious disease just before he started college. He was to play football for Ole Miss. The surgery he had to have ended his football career.

Peyton went to Isidore Newman School from kindergarten through high school and earned good grades. In 1991, he became the quarterback for the school's **varsity** team. Cooper

Peyton had dreamed of being at Ole Miss with his brother Cooper. When that dream came apart, he decided to start fresh at the University of Tennessee.

was his favorite **wide receiver.** Before Peyton got the ball, he'd make secret hand signals to his brother. Cooper knew exactly where to run, and Peyton would throw him the ball.

Peyton played quarterback for the varsity for three years. During that time, he led Isidore Newman to thirty-five wins and just five losses. Many colleges wanted Peyton to play football for their teams. He picked the University of Tennessee in Knoxville.

Peyton deeply respected his father *(right)*. He wanted to live up to Archie's college success.

STUDENT OF THE GAME

Peyton was proud to wear the orange-and-white uniform of the Tennessee Volunteers. In 1994, as a freshman, he was the **third-string** quarterback. Even though he didn't play yet, he practiced hard. He wanted to be ready to play if the team needed him. Peyton was needed sooner than anyone expected.

In the first game of the season, the first-string, or starting, quarterback got hurt. Two weeks later, the second-string quarterback got hurt too. Suddenly, Peyton was the team's quarterback.

Peyton was named the starting quarterback in his first year at the University of Tennessee.

15

Peyton worked hard to learn the plays that would bring his team victory.

In his first game, he was careful not to throw an **interception.** The Volunteers won, 10–9. Peyton grew more confident. He led his team to six wins in its last seven games. He even guided the Volunteers to a 45–23 win over Virginia Tech in the Gator Bowl.

Peyton was a serious college student who earned good grades. He also studied the football team's **playbook** and looked at **game films.** Peyton's hard work paid off. In the 1995 season, he set team records for **completions** and yards passing. The University of Tennessee was named one of the best teams in the country.

Tennessee head coach Phillip Fulmer *(left)* worked with Peyton throughout his time at the University of Tennessee.

By 1996, Peyton had become a statewide hero. When people saw him at restaurants or malls, they chanted his name. The town of Knoxville, Tennessee, named a street Peyton Manning Pass. Peyton was uncomfortable with all the fuss. In 1997, his senior season, he led the Volunteers to an 11–1 record. They earned the right to play in the Orange Bowl.

College bowl games take place after the regular season is over. They show off the country's best teams.

Peyton holds up the jersey of the Indianapolis Colts, the team that drafted him in 1998.

ALL-PRO THROWER

Peyton knew he wanted to play in the NFL after he finished college in 1998. Many football experts thought he was sure to be one of the first players chosen in the 1998 NFL **Draft.** The Indianapolis Colts had the first pick, and they chose Peyton.

The Colts offered Peyton a **contract** for $48 million to play for them for six years. Peyton agreed and immediately set up the PeyBack Foundation. This group would give money to people in need.

But Peyton had a big job ahead. The Colts were losers. They had won just three of sixteen games in the 1997 season. Most **rookie** quarterbacks don't play in their first year, but the Colts really needed Peyton's help.

Peyton's first season was tough. Here, he's getting tackled by a member of the New York Jets.

At training camp, before the start of his second season, Peyton ran sprints to become faster and more fit.

He struggled, winning just three games in the 1998 season. "It was frustrating," Peyton said. "But you can either sit there and feel sorry for yourself or learn from it and do something about it."

Peyton worked harder than ever to get himself ready for the 1999 season. He lifted weights and ran sprints. He memorized the team playbook—not just the plays for the quarterback but every play in the book. Could he help his team be a winner?

Peyton studied hard to learn the Colts'
playbook. Soon his coaches trusted him
to change plays on the field.

Peyton focused on playing well in the 1999
season. He turned the Colts into winners.
Indianapolis's 13–3 record was the biggest
improvement in NFL history. Six of the wins
were fourth-quarter **comebacks,** showing that

Peyton was calm in the final minutes. The Colts even made it to the NFL **playoffs** but lost the first playoff game.

They won ten games in the 2000 season to reach the playoffs again. Unfortunately, they lost again. The Colts had a worse season in 2001, with six wins and ten losses. In the 2002 season, Peyton's team reached the postseason yet again. This time, the Colts lost to the New York Jets. Indianapolis went to the playoffs in 2003, 2004, and 2005. Each time they lost and failed to reach the Super Bowl. Indianapolis put all of these playoff losses behind them after the 2006 season. The Colts were Super Bowl champions, and Peyton was the MVP of the game.

Peyton and his brother Eli *(right)* with their father, Archie *(center)*.

HOMETOWN HERO

Peyton Manning is one of the most successful and well-paid players in the NFL. But the money and the fame haven't lessened his interest in giving back to the community. He and his wife Ashley care deeply about all children. The PeyBack Foundation gives hundreds of thousands of dollars every year to Toys for Tots and Boys and Girls Clubs.

"I try to be a person that people can look up to," Peyton says. "I'm not doing it for any fake reasons. That's the person I want to be. My parents taught me to do the right thing, and that's what I try to do."

In August 2005, Hurricane Katrina almost destroyed Peyton's hometown of New Orleans. Many people lost their lives. Homes and businesses were ruined across the city and the state.

Many parts of New Orleans were damaged by Hurricane Katrina.

This tragedy deeply affected the Manning family. Peyton wanted to help his hometown. "The whole town is like family, so it's very much a personal issue," he said.

Peyton and his younger brother Eli, quarterback of the NFL's New York Giants, decided to do something. They knew that people in New Orleans and other parts of Louisiana were desperate for things like baby food and water. So Peyton and Eli helped the American Red Cross load an airplane with supplies. They even flew to Baton Rouge,

Louisiana, to help unload the supplies. They also visited shelters where people who had lost their homes in the storm were staying.

After finally winning the Super Bowl, Peyton was on top of the world. Fans everywhere had watched his amazing play in the biggest football game of the year. He was very popular. A few days after the game, Peyton appeared on the *Late Show with David Letterman*. A few weeks later he hosted *Saturday Night Live*.

Peyton and his brother Eli *(center)* visited American Red Cross shelters in Louisiana after Hurricane Katrina.

Peyton celebrates the Colts' Super Bowl victory with teammates and fans in Indianapolis.

Peyton was having a great time, but football was never far from his mind. Hard work made him a Super Bowl MVP, and he will keep working hard. Peyton plans to be back on the field before long. "We're going to work in March, and we're going to be better because of this," he said. How many Super Bowls can Peyton and his teammates win? With their star quarterback leading the way, the sky is the limit for the Colts.

Selected Career Highlights

2007   Named Super Bowl MVP
Named Walter Payton NFL Man of the Year

2006   Led all quarterbacks with 31 touchdown passes

2005   Led all players in votes for 2006 Pro Bowl
Named Walter Payton NFL Man of the Year

2004   Named NFL Quarterback of the Year by
National Quarterback Club
Won ESPY award as Best NFL Player
Set the record for most touchdown passes in a single season

2003   Named NFL co-MVP
Named NFL Player of the Year by Maxwell Football Club
Set NFL record for throwing at least twenty-five touchdown passes
in six straight seasons
Selected to Pro Bowl for fourth time

2002   Selected to Pro Bowl for third time

2001   Led the American Football Conference (AFC) in passing yards

2000   Broke team record for touchdown passes in a season, with
thirty-three
Became fifth quarterback in NFL history to pass for over 4,000
yards in a season
Selected to Pro Bowl for second time

1999   Selected to Pro Bowl for first time

1998   Selected first in the NFL draft

1997   Won the Sullivan Award, given each year to the nation's top
amateur athlete
Finished college career with thirty-three school records and two
NCAA records

1996   Became first Tennessee quarterback to pass for more than 3,000
yards in a season

1995   Selected Associated Press third team All-America
Set an NCAA record for lowest interception rate in a season

1994   Named Southeastern Conference Freshman of the Year

Glossary

comeback: a win in the final minutes of a game after a team has been losing

completion: the catch of a pass from the quaterback

contract: a written deal signed by a player and his or her team. The player agrees to play for the team for a stated number of years. The team agrees to pay the player a stated amount of money.

defense: the team of eleven players that doesn't have the football. The defense tries to stop the other team from scoring.

draft: a yearly event in which all professional teams in a sport are given the chance to pick new players from a selected group

end zone: the area beyond the goal line. To score, a team tries to get the ball into the other team's end zone.

field goal: a successful kick over the U-shaped upright poles. A field goal is worth three points.

fumble: a football that is dropped on the ground during a game that any player can recover.

game film: a videotape of a game that players and coaches can study

goal line: the line at the edge of the end zone that a team crosses to score points

interception: a pass that is caught by a person on the defense. An interception results in the opposing team getting control of the ball.

playbook: a book that describes plays a team will use in games

playoffs: a series of games played after the regular season has ended

rookie: a player who is playing his or her first season

third-string: the name given to the third player at a certain position. The first-string player is the starting player. The second-string player replaces the first-string player and so on.

touchdown: a score in which the team with the ball crosses its opponent's goal line. A touchdown is worth six points.

varsity: the school team made up of the most experienced or best players

wide receiver: a player who catches passes, mainly for a big gain

Further Reading & Websites

Hyams, Jimmy. *Peyton Manning: Primed and Ready*. Shawnee Mission, KS: Addax Publishing Group, 1998.

Manning, Peyton, and Archie Manning. *Manning: A Father, His Sons and a Football Legacy*. New York: HarperEntertainment, 2000.

Rappoport, Ken. *Super Sports Star Peyton Manning*. Berkeley Heights, NJ: Enslow Publishers, Inc., 2003.

Savage, Jeff. *Peyton Manning: Precision Passer*. Minneapolis: Lerner Publications Company, 2001.

Stewart, Mark. *Peyton Manning: Rising Son*. Minneapolis: Millbrook Press, 2000.

Wilner, Barry. *Peyton Manning*. Berkeley Heights, NJ: Enslow Publishers, Inc., 2003.

Official NFL Site
http://www.nfl.com
The official National Football League website that provides fans with game action, biographies of players, and information about football.

Peyton's Website
http://www.peytonmanning.com
Peyton's official website, featuring trivia, photos, and information about Peyton and his PeyBack Foundation.

Sports Illustrated for Kids
http://www.sikids.com
The *Sports Illustrated for Kids* website that covers all sports, including football.

Index

Photo Acknowledgments

Photographs are used with the permission of: © Brian Bahr/Getty Images, p. 4; © Gary I. Rothstein/Icon SMI, p. 5; © Eliot J. Schechter/Getty Images, p. 6; AP Photo/David J. Phillip, p. 7; AP Photo/Kevork Djansezian, p. 8; © Tom Hauck/Getty Images, p. 9; © University of Mississippi, p. 10; © Bettmann/CORBIS, p. 11; © Scott Halleran/Allsport/Getty Images, p. 13; © Jamie Squire/Getty Images, pp. 14, 19; © Jonathan Daniel/Allsport/Getty Images, p. 15; AP Photo/Mark Humphrey, p. 16; © Reuters/CORBIS, p. 17; © Al Bello/Getty Images, p. 20; © Brent Smith/Reuters/CORBIS, pp. 21, 22; © Sporting News/Icon SMI, p. 24; Marty Bahamonde/FEMA, p. 25; REUTERS/Allen Fredrickson, p. 26; © Allen Fredrickson/Reuters/CORBIS, p. 27; © Tasos Katopodis/Getty Images, p. 28; © Rob Tringali/SportsChrome, p. 29.

Cover image: © Jonathan Daniel/Getty Images